IMAGES
of America

DENALI NATIONAL
PARK AND PRESERVE

ON THE COVER: Herschel Parker leads this rope team trying to find a route to the summit in 1910. In lieu of today's harnesses and kernmantle ropes, early mountaineers climbed using hemp ropes they wrapped around their waists for protection in the event of a fall. (Library of Congress.)

IMAGES
of America

DENALI NATIONAL PARK AND PRESERVE

Shelby Carpenter

ARCADIA
PUBLISHING

Published by Arcadia Publishing
Charleston, South Carolina

Printed in the United States of America

Library of Congress Control Number: 2014936556

For all general information, please contact Arcadia Publishing:
Telephone 843-853-2070
Fax 843-853-0044
E-mail sales@arcadiapublishing.com
For customer service and orders:
Toll-Free 1-888-313-2665

Visit us on the Internet at www.arcadiapublishing.com

I dedicate this book to my brother, Ross—the single best guy I know.

CONTENTS

ACKNOWLEDGMENTS

I would first like to thank those who graciously provided me with the historical images featured in this book. While some of the photographs are from my own climbing trips in the Alaska Range, many come from Candy Waugaman—a private collector in Fairbanks, Alaska—and the archivists and historians at Denali National Park and Preserve (DENA). Candy was kind enough to welcome me into her home and share her beautiful collection with me, and without her help, I could not have completed this book. Kim Arthur and others at the National Park Service were similarly giving of their knowledge and time. I must also thank the Library of Congress for its voluminous collection of historical images available to the public.

Additionally, I would like to thank Tom Walker, Frank Norris, Jane Bryant, and the other writers, climbers, and historians whose work I relied on while writing the text for this book; my friends and family for supporting me throughout this endeavor; and Jeff Ruetsche at Arcadia Publishing for entrusting me with this project.

INTRODUCTION

After floating down the Tanana River and traveling through the Kantishna Hills, James Wickersham ascended the Peters Glacier with four others to make the first recorded attempt to climb Denali. They reached the Jeffrey Glacier only to find themselves beneath a 14,000-foot wall of ice. Realizing there was no way they could ascend the ice face towering above them, the disheartened climbers had to descend the mountain and return to Fairbanks in defeat.

Wickersham is a prime example of the leaders of early Denali climbs, who tended not only to be climbers but also members of the upper class. In Wickersham's case, he moved to Alaska from Washington to work as a judge in Alaska's Third Judicial District, where he had to rule on legal matters across 300,000 square miles of territory. During his Denali expedition Wickersham mined for gold on Chitsia Creek and, after filing his mining claims, inadvertently set off the Kantishna gold rush. In addition to his judicial, climbing, and mining exploits, Wickersham would also become Alaska's first delegate to Congress in 1908.

Wickersham was just one among dozens of climbers who made the first attempts on Denali. Dr. Frederick Cook would also try—and fail—to climb the mountain just a few weeks after Wickersham's 1903 expedition. In 1906, Cook returned to try again, with Belmore Browne, Herschel Parker, and Edward Barrill, and claimed to have reached the summit after leaving Browne and Parker behind. However, many Alaskans were skeptical of Cook's boasting, and Browne and Parker returned on their own in 1910 to gather evidence to disprove Cook's claim.

One of the most well-known early climbs is the so-called Sourdough Expedition in 1910. The team, composed of four miners from Fairbanks, stood in stark contrast to the high-class leaders of other climbs like Wickersham and Cook. While the men did not climb the taller south peak on Denali, they did reach the top of the north peak and planted a 14-foot spruce pole, which they believed could be seen with a very powerful telescope from Fairbanks and serve as proof of their ascent.

In 1913, Hudson Stuck and his partners Harry Karstens, who would later become superintendent of the park, Walter Harper, and Robert Tatum made the first successful ascent of the south peak.

While these early climbers are notable, they made up just a tiny fraction of visitors and settlers in Denali. Athabascan Native culture has existed as a cultural and linguistic tradition in Alaska for approximately 7,000 years, and five different groups of Athabascan Natives lived in the area that was to become the park for several hundred years before white settlers arrived.

It was the Kantishna gold rush in 1905 that brought thousands of new miners, prospectors, and other settlers to the region. A series of other rushes—including the Klondike gold rush in the late 1890s and the Nome gold strike in 1899—had drawn prospectors and other hopefuls up to Alaska from the Lower 48. Many Kantishna miners and prospectors were veterans of these other rushes.

As prospectors flowed into the area, they began to have a serious environmental impact through game hunting. Hunters started to pick off Dall sheep, caribou, and other species to feed the gold rushers, and the lack of any regulations meant these large mammals could easily go extinct as the Great Plains bison nearly had.

It was this danger of species eradication, in fact, that led to the first efforts to create Denali National Park and Preserve. Charles Sheldon, a railroad tycoon and East Coast conservationist, traveled to Alaska to document the life cycle of Dall sheep in 1906. After spending a summer in the region, he returned to spend the winter of 1907–1908 in a cabin with Harry Karstens observing, recording, and gathering specimens of animals and plants. Sheldon would become one of the biggest advocates of the park as a way to protect game species like Dall sheep from extinction.

Sheldon enlisted the support of Wickersham, and at their urging Congress passed a bill to create Mount McKinley National Park. Pres. Woodrow Wilson signed the bill into law on February 26, 1917. The new park encompassed almost 1.6 million acres and did not yet have any funding for rangers or other staff.

Harry Karstens—the man who had participated in the Stuck expedition to climb Denali, and who stayed with Charles Sheldon during his Dall sheep research—would become the park's first superintendent. Karstens oversaw the opening of tourism operations and the hiring of the park's first rangers. He also supervised the development of the first roads into the park and the construction of the park headquarters, ranger cabins, dog kennels, and other early structures.

Today, over 1,000 climbers come to attempt the West Buttress route on Denali each year, and others go to conquer peaks in the Ruth Gorge, Little Switzerland, on Mount Foraker, or other popular climbing areas in the Alaska Range that are protected under the umbrella of Denali National Park and Preserve. While the park may have started as a way to protect Dall sheep, it now serves as an international hub of alpine climbing.

What follows is a history of Denali National Park and Preserve told through historic images and captions. This book is by no means an authoritative history of the park, but rather a series of vignettes that provide a sense of place, and of history. This is a story that runs across turbulent rivers, through the halls of Congress and the offices of businessmen, down deep into mines in the Kantishna Hills, and to the top of the highest peak in North America. Enjoy the journey.

This panoramic photograph from the 1950s captures some of the beauty and grandeur of Denali. Note the floatplane at the far left. Alaska's bush pilots would play a major role in the exploration

of the park during the first half of the 20th century. (Library of Congress.)

One

THE KANTISHNA
GOLD RUSH

Mt. McKinley
from
Stony Point

Here is the heart
of Mt. McKinley
National Park,
the second largest
national park
under the American
flag. The park is
a haven for Grizzly
bears, herds of
Caribou, Dall
sheep, foxes,
Moose and other
wild game.

It has 112 species
of birds and 35
varieties of
animals in addition
to thousands of
wildflowers.
Mt. McKinley
National
Park
Alaska
E-4764

At 20,237 feet, Denali is the tallest peak in North America. In the heart of the Alaska Range, the mountain is the high point of a massive cordillera running from the Alaska-Canada border all the way through the Aleutian Islands. Denali is surrounded by numerous other high peaks 10,000 feet and taller, including Mount Foraker, which, at 17,400 feet, is the sixth-highest mountain on the continent. (Candy Waugaman collection.)

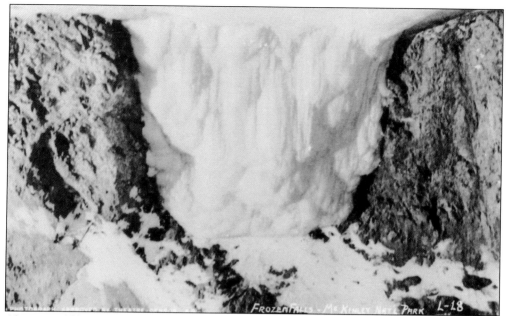

Almost one-fifth of the park is covered with snow year-round. Glaciers, snowfields, and ice-encrusted peaks characterize the south side of the Alaska Range, whereas the north side of the range has consistently lower elevations and is less snowy. The more mild conditions on the north side of the range mean that it is home to a greater variety of wildlife than the area to the south. (Candy Waugaman collection.)

Denali National Park and Preserve is home to 25 species of mammals, including Dall sheep, caribou, wolves, grizzly bears, moose, lynx, red foxes, and porcupines. It is also the habitat for 166 different species of bird, 15 species of fish, and even one species of amphibian. (Candy Waugaman collection.)

Various Native populations have lived within the boundaries of today's park since 7,000 years ago, and the earliest known habitation sites just outside the park boundaries are 11,000 years old. The dominant Native tradition in the area is the Athabascan culture. Five groups of Athabascan-speaking Indians have lived in Denali for the past several hundred years—the Dena'ina, the Ahtna, the Koyukon, the Upper Kuskokwim, and the Lower Tanana. (Candy Waugaman collection.)

The Lower Tanana people lived in villages along the Tanana River. Those villages were located in what is today the northeastern part of Denali National Park and Preserve and the city of Fairbanks. (Candy Waugaman collection.)

When white settlers came to the area, among their numbers were missionaries with the mandate to convert Alaska Native peoples to Christianity. This patronizing informational booklet describes the day-to-day lives of Alaska Native children for the benefit of white Christians looking to support missionary efforts. (Candy Waugaman collection.)

After the Panic of 1893, a nationwide financial crisis that left thousands starving and destitute, many poor Americans were eager to jump at the first chance of wealth, however unlikely that chance might be. Gold fever brought the hungry and the hopeful—like the unidentified prospectors featured in this image—to Alaska in search of wealth. (Candy Waugaman collection.)

In August 1896, a man named George Carmack along with two partners, Tagish Charlie and Skookum Jim, discovered fantastic quantities of gold in a tributary of the Klondike River. Word of their strike quickly spread and, in 1897 alone, more than one hundred thousand people would head for the Klondike unaware that the entire stream had already been staked by the end of August 1896. (Candy Waugaman collection.)

The Klondike gold rush and subsequent rushes did bring fantastic wealth, but only for the earliest prospectors. Others who followed years or even months after an initial strike typically arrived to find the best mining claims already staked by the first arrivals. These unlucky hopefuls were left to find other ways to make ends meet—or to turn to drink in the saloons that sprang up in practically every new boomtown. (Candy Waugaman collection.)

To reach the Klondike, many prospectors would take a steamer from Seattle to Skagway. From Skagway, they would attempt to travel the difficult White Pass or Chilkoot Trails to Dawson. They would then load up horses or hire packers to transport their mining equipment and as much food and supplies as they could afford to the mining and prospecting camps. (Candy Waugaman collection.)

With only the most basic supplies at hand, many prospectors lived in canvas tents or in cabins built from logs they cut and laid themselves. In order to survive, those who were not lucky enough to strike it rich in the initial rush were forced to find work doing menial labor—often for other prospectors who did in fact have valuable claims. (Candy Waugaman collection.)

In any given boomtown, foodstuffs were only available at the most outrageously inflated prices. Living in simple cabins, prospectors often subsisted only on flour, bacon, and beans along with a few other niceties like sugar, salt, and milk. (Candy Waugaman collection.)

Despite outstanding odds against success, prospectors continued to flow into Alaska by the thousands from the time gold was discovered on the Klondike in 1896 through the early 1900s, when the

Kantishna gold rush brought prospectors to the Denali area. (Candy Waugaman collection.)

19

In this image, Pres. William McKinley holds a procession in Golden Gate Park in San Francisco in 1901. The mountain—known today alternately as Denali and as Mount McKinley—entered the American lexicon when prospector William Dickey referred to the peak as Mount McKinley to honor the then Ohio governor in his presidential bid. (Library of Congress.)

After the federal government accepted Dickey's naming, efforts to officially change the name from Mount McKinley to Denali by some Alaskans met with stiff resistance from public officials in Ohio. While most Alaskans prefer the Athabascan name Denali, it is still called Mount McKinley on the books. (Candy Waugaman collection.)

In this 1917 image, prospector W.G. Jack stands before a cabin near Caribou Creek. During the Kantishna gold rush, prospectors first headed to Glacier Creek before exploring Moose Creek and Caribou Creek nearby. (Candy Waugaman collection.)

This is the cabin where Charles McGonagall, one of the members of the Sourdough Expedition, lived. He came to Alaska from Chicago in 1896. First, he floated the Yukon in search of gold on the Fortymile River, and he later carried mail from the town of Fortymile to Fort Yukon. When miners struck gold in Nome in 1900, McGonagall rushed towards the strike only to end up quarantined 50 miles away from his destination due to a smallpox epidemic. Apart from taking part in the Sourdough Expedition, he is also known for discovering the eponymous McGonagall Pass. (Candy Waugaman collection.)

W.G. Jack (left) and two unidentified men stand in front of a cabin belonging to Joe Quigley, a prospector legendary not only for his own doings but also for those of his wife, Fannie Quigley. After years of dog-mushing and prospecting, the Quigleys would become long-term residents of the Kantishna Hills. (Candy Waugaman collection.)

This is another image of the cabin where Joe Quigley lived. He was among the first prospectors to explore the area around the Kantishna River after Wickersham discovered gold in Chitsia Creek. (DENA 3509.)

In the far left of this image stands Fannie Quigley. Fannie and Joe Quigley were perhaps the most well-known couple to settle in the Kantishna. Fannie was born Fannie Sedlacek in 1870 on a homestead in Nebraska and grew up speaking Czech. She later learned English as she worked her way west and headed for the Klondike in search of gold. She worked various jobs, including stints as a dance-hall girl and a cook, before getting a miner's certificate to stake her own claims for gold. Also pictured here, from left to right, are a Dr. Sutherland, two unidentified miners, W.G. Jack, and John Clark. (Candy Waugaman collection.)

Here, Joe Quigley is seen running supplies by dogsled from Fairbanks to Kantishna. Originally from Pennsylvania, Quigley came to Alaska in 1891 and quickly became a veteran of the area's numerous gold rushes. He and Fannie Sedlacek shared chores and breaking trail during their years as travel partners prior to their marriage. (DENA 3511.)

This is an image of Joe and Fannie Quigley's cabin in Kantishna after it was rehabilitated. While most prospectors abandoned the area when the Kantishna gold rush dissipated, the Quigleys were two of a handful of prospectors who remained to eke out a living off the land. (Library of Congress.)

While gold strikes drew settlers to the region, prospecting also brought with it a dark side—a greater impact on the land these early prospectors explored. Miners and prospectors were the source of a host of environmental issues, including the unregulated slaughter of wildlife, the mass cutting of trees to build cabins, and the damming of rivers to facilitate mining. (Candy Waugaman collection.)

When white settlers arrived, they found Denali to be home to a number of large game species, including caribou, moose, grizzly bears, wolves, and Dall sheep. These large mammals in particular became the target not only of subsistence hunters but also of market hunters looking to sell meat to the mining camps. (Library of Congress.)

MOUNTAIN SHEEP IN McKINLEY PARK ALASKA

Dall sheep was one northern species that quickly came under threat from excessive hunting. At the time, the sheep were a relative mystery to naturalists and scientists in the Lower 48, but to hunters they were an easy and ample source of food. (Candy Waugaman collection.)

In an area with no domesticated meat industry to supply miners, it was not long before market hunters entered to fill the farming void. The impact of game hunting started to draw national attention, and the East Coast hunter-naturalist Charles Sheldon would enter the fray to promote the idea of a game preserve. (Candy Waugaman collection.)

These market hunters did provide a service to prospectors and other early settlers who relied on the availability of game meat for sustenance. But at the same time, in the absence of any kind of regulation or protection, it would be easy enough for these animals to share the same fate as the Great Plains bison, which nearly went extinct. (Candy Waugaman collection.)

Charles Alexander Sheldon, an East Coast conservationist who had become wealthy from railroad and mining investments, eventually came to Alaska in the summer of 1906 to study the Dall sheep for the US Biological Survey. Part of Sheldon's study involved collecting specimens—such as hides and skulls of the sheep—and taking various measurements. (DENA 1966.)

Originally from Chicago, Henry Peter Karstens, called Harry, came to Alaska in 1897 as part of the Klondike gold rush. This undated photograph features a buggy from the White Pass Yukon route, one of the routes used to get to Dawson during the Klondike gold rush. (Candy Waugaman collection.)

Because Karstens and his partner lacked the supplies and the funds to mine on their own, they started working as packers in Skagway. Karstens developed strong arctic survival skills and the ability to mush dogs. This 1916 image depicts a typical dog team like the one Karstens would have used. He would later work as a mail carrier in rural Alaska and also take part in the first successful climb of Denali. Karstens also served as Sheldon's friend and guide as he studied Dall sheep in the area that would become the park. (Library of Congress.)

For his 1906 trip, Sheldon hired Karstens and another packer to take him through the wilds of Denali to study Dall sheep and other animals in the area. That July, Sheldon got his first view of Denali near Wonder Lake, featured in this image. He vowed to return to the area the following year to pursue a more in-depth study of the Dall sheep. (Candy Waugaman collection.)

Karstens and Sheldon returned to Denali in August 1907 and built a cabin on the Toklat River. It was during his year in Denali with Karstens that Sheldon began to dream of a wildlife refuge to protect Dall sheep and other wildlife from excessive hunting. This image shows the remains of the cabin where Karstens and Sheldon lived. (DENA 21225.)

This photograph is of a party on Harry Karstens's boat. Apart from his involvement with Sheldon, Karstens is also known for taking part in the first successful expedition to climb Denali. While the official team leader was Hudson Stuck, Karstens was the primary climber bringing arctic-survival and mountaineering skills to the group. (Candy Waugaman collection.)

Sheldon enlisted Judge Wickersham to advocate for the protection of Denali wildlife. Conservation was still a new concept at the beginning of the 20th century. The National Park Service itself would not be established until 1916, and the US Army managed the few parks that did exist. The National Forest Service did not exist yet either, though there were a handful of forest preserves across the country. This made Sheldon and Wickersham unusual actors on the national stage in advocating for a game preserve in a time when others of their generation thought only of hunting those species to the max. (Both, Candy Waugaman collection.)

This early-20th-century image, showing two sled dog teams at the foot of the mountain, captures some of the scale of Denali and the daunting challenge facing those first climbers who would attempt to reach its summit. (Library of Congress.)

Two

EARLY CLIMBING

This photograph of Judge James Wickersham (second row, third from right) with Alaska Native leaders was taken in the early 1900s. Born in Patoka, Illinois, in 1857, Wickersham eventually became city attorney for Tacoma, Washington. In 1900, he was appointed by President McKinley to serve as judge for Alaska's Third Judicial District, which spanned 300,000 square miles throughout the territory and was composed mainly of Alaska Native residents. Wickersham would later be renowned for making the first known attempt to climb Denali. (Library of Congress.)

After arriving in Alaska, Wickersham (left) built a log cabin for his wife and seven-year-old son. In 1902, his son would die of typhoid fever, but despite this personal tragedy, he began plotting his ascent of Denali for 1903. (Library of Congress.)

To begin its expedition, Wickersham's
team floated down the Tanana River
to the Kantishna River. Then, the men
followed the Kantishna to the Toklat and
headed southwest to make their attempt
via the Peters Glacier. Once there, they
were met by a seemingly impassable
14,000-foot wall of ice, today called the
Wickersham Wall, blocking their access
to the mountain's north peak and forcing
them to turn around. (Library of Congress.)

Wickersham's journey did have one
unintended result—a gold rush. In the
course of their trip, the men discovered gold
in Chitsia Creek and filed mining claims
with the court. Once other prospectors
heard the news and discovered more
gold in nearby creek, the Kantishna gold
rush ensued. (Library of Congress.)

Wickersham sits at the center of this image from 1915. He became Alaska's first delegate to Congress in 1909 after serving as a district court judge in Fairbanks. With the urging of Charles Sheldon, Wickersham became an ardent supporter of the creation of the park. (Candy Waugaman collection.)

Dr. Frederick Cook—featured here in a fur coat and pants—attempted to climb Denali just a few weeks after Wickersham in 1903. He made it as high as 11,000 feet on the Peters Glacier before retreating. He also returned in 1906 with Belmore Browne, Edward Barrill, and Herschel C. Parker and claimed to have reached the summit on his own after leaving behind his companions. (Library of Congress.)

Cook's claim of reaching the summit was met with support by some and furious speculation by others. He would also later claim, falsely, to have reached the North Pole in 1909. This image is of Cook and one of his companions near an igloo on their North Pole trek. Adm. Robert Peary, who also claimed to have reached the North Pole in 1909, would tell the world that he had not seen Cook near the pole and that his assertion must be false. (Library of Congress.)

Frederick Cook was honored at a banquet held by the Arctic Club of America in 1909. Peary's accusations that Cook was a fraud would invite speculation not only into his polar expedition, but also to his claim to have summited Denali. His former detractors, of course, weighed in—Wickersham would slam Cook as a liar in his book *Old Yukon: Tales, Trails and Trials*. Edward Barrill, one of Cook's climbing companions, would later recant his story in support of Cook having reached the summit. (Both, Library of Congress.)

Herschel C. Parker was a physics professor at Columbia University. Part of the infamous 1906 attempt led by Dr. Cook, Parker met his future climbing partner, Belmore Browne, by chance in the smoking parlor of a passenger train, and they would be friends for the next 40 years. (Library of Congress.)

This image of Mrs. H.C. Parker near Denali dates from the early 1900s. Herschel Parker, her husband, would return in 1910 with Belmore Browne and Merl LaVoy to attempt the mountain

and gather proof that Cook's claim to the summit was false. (Library of Congress.)

Once the controversy erupted about Cook's North Pole expedition, Browne and Parker finally had the support they needed from the public, much of which had favored Cook, to take an expedition and disprove his claim. The Explorers Club and the American Geographical Society jumped in to support their attempt to climb Denali and document the impossibility of Cook's claim of a successful ascent. (Library of Congress.)

Browne, Parker, and LaVoy were forced by avalanche and crevasse hazard to turn back at the west fork of the Ruth Glacier. While they failed to reach Denali's summit, their own challenges served as evidence that Cook could not have reached the summit in the short time frame he had claimed. (Library of Congress.)

Herschel Parker is seen here on the lead trying to find a route to the summit on Denali. In lieu of today's harnesses and kernmantle ropes, early mountaineers climbed on hemp ropes that they wrapped around their waists for protection in the event of a fall. The climber to the right of the image holds his ice ax on his uphill side and the rope on his downhill side, which is still a standard practice today. These climbers also wear an early version of the crampons climbers strap to their boots for traction on the ice; they were called "ice-creepers" rather than crampons and were often homemade. (Library of Congress.)

The First Authentic Picture of Mount McKinley, Alaska. 20,300 ft. high.
taken by M. Lavoy, a member of the Parker-Browne Ex-
dition of 1910 from Explorers' Peak, 90 feet high.
pyright 1910, by M. La Voy.

One notable outcome of the 1910 Parker-Browne-LaVoy expedition, apart from helping to disprove Cook's claim to the summit, was bringing back the first known photograph of the mountain's summit. LaVoy took this image, which was published upon the group's return. (Candy Waugaman collection.)

Three

THE FIRST YEARS
OF THE PARK

Alaska officially became a US territory when Congress passed the Second Organic Act in 1912. This act also established the Alaska Railroad Commission, which was charged with reporting on the best potential rail route through Alaska's interior. The possibility of a rail line increased pressure on conservationists to find ways to protect game species, which would be threatened by the influx of travelers and settlers the new railroad would bring. (Candy Waugaman collection.)

Tickets to Alaska permit stopover to visit Mt. McKinley National Park. For further information regarding trips into the Park, address

MT. McKINLEY ALASKA 20,300 FEET

MOUNTAIN SHEEP ALASKA

PACK TRAIN ENROUTE

Game Protected in the Park. Fine Hunting Grounds to the Eastward

MT. McKINLEY TOURIST & TRANSPORTATION CO., Inc.
McKinley Park, Alaska

Hunting Parties Should Make Arrangements in Advance

On March 12, 1914, Congress passed the Alaska Railroad Act and funded the creation of a rail line. The commission considered various routes, and in April 1915, President Wilson ordered the creation of a route from Seward to Fairbanks in an executive order. (Candy Waugaman collection.)

MT. McKINLEY PARK ROUTE
TRAIN SCHEDULES
Anchorage to Fairbanks

NORTH — READ DOWN					SOUTH — READ UP	
TRAIN NO. 8 TU-WED	TRAIN NO. 6 SAT	MILES FROM SEWARD	MAIN LINE	ELEVATION	TRAIN NO. 5 SUN	TRAIN NO. 7 WED-TH
8:00	9:00	114.3	Lv Anchorage (R.R. Headquarters) ....Ar	38	s8:45	s8:45
f8:08	f9:08	117.0	" Fort Richardson (Elmendorf Air Force Base to left; Fort Richardson to right)			
f8:15	f9:15	119.1	" Whitney	140	f8:32	f8:29
f8:30	f9:30	126.6	" Eagle River (Eagle River Canyon)	222	f8:27	f8:27
f8:50	f9:50	136.3	" Birchwood (Peters Creek)	197	f8:10	f8:09
f9:00	f10:00	141.2	" Eklutna (Indian Village)	92	f7:50	f7:48
s9:20	s10:18	150.7	" Matanuska (Junction to Palmer farms and coal mines)	50	f7:40	f7:38
				36	s7:22	s7:19
s9:44	s10:42	159.8	" Wasilla (to Willow Creek Gold Area)	339	s7:00	s6:57
f9:55	f10:53	166.5	" Pittman	300	f6:49	f6:46
f10:09	f11:07	174.9	" Houston (Little Susitna River)	246	f6:35	f6:32
f10:16	f11:14	180.7	" Nancy (Lake Nancy—Summer Cabins)	236	f6:22	f6:20
s10:30	s11:25	185.7	" Willow (Willow Creek)	232	s6:15	s6:12
f10:35	f11:30	190.5	" Little Willow	175	f6:05	f5:59
f10:44	f11:39	193.9	" Kashwitna	236	f6:00	f5:55
f11:00	f11:55	202.3	" Caswell (Sheep Creek)	246	f5:45	f5:40
		207.8	" Goose Creek	240		
f11:14	f12:09	209.3	" Montana (Homesteads)	282	f5:32	f5:27
		211.0	" Montana Creek	260		
f11:24	f12:19	215.3	" Sunshine	328	f5:21	f5:16
		221.3	" Fish Lake	310		
s11:47	s12:39	226.7	" Talkeetna** (To Cache Creek Mining District)	354	s5:01	s4:56
f12:03	f12:55	236.2	" Chase	461	f4:44	f4:39
f12:29	f1:20	248.5	" Curry (Former Important R.R. Terminal)	546	f4:23	f4:18
f12:46	f1:37	257.7	" Sherman	621	f4:00	f3:53
f12:56	f1:47	263.2	" Gold Creek	731	f3:48	f3:41
f1:07	f1:58	268.4	" Canyon (Indian River)	879	f3:38	f3:31
f1:23	f2:13	273.8	" Chulitna (Summit Lake)	1280	f3:27	f3:19
f1:48	f2:35	281.4	" Hurricane (Hurricane Gulch)	1688	f3:12	f3:04
f2:08	f2:55	288.7	" Honolulu	1456	f2:55	f2:47
f2:24	f3:11	297.1	" Colorado (Former Mining District)	1954	f2:40	f2:32
f2:38	f3:25	304.3	" Broad Pass (Continental Divide Six Miles North)	2127	f2:29	f2:21
s2:53	s3:40	312.5	" Summit	2337	s2:16	s2:08
s3:07	s3:54	319.5	" Cantwell (Cantwell River)	2212	s2:03	s1:55
f3:22	f4:09	326.7	" Windy (Panorama Mountain)	2056	f1:49	f1:41
f3:38	f4:25	334.4	" Carlo (Carlo Creek)	1957	f1:33	f1:25
f3:58	f4:45	343.7	" Lagoon	1890	f1:14	f1:06
s4:09	s4:55	347.9	" McKinley Park (Gateway to Mt. McKinley National Park)	1732	s1:04	s12:56
f4:39	f5:25	355.7	" Garner	1432	f12:34	f12:25
s4:49	s5:35	358.1	Ar Healy** (Junction to Coal Mines) Lv	1368	12:25	12:25
5:45	5:54	358.1	Lv Healy ....Ar	1368	s12:16	s12:05
f5:15	f5:54	363.3	" Lignite	1176	f12:07	f11:55
f5:28	f6:06	371.2	" Ferry	1006	f11:55	f11:42
f5:44	f6:21	381.2	" Browne	810	f11:40	f11:24
s6:01	s6:40	392.9	" Clear Site	597	s11:21	s11:07
f6:17	f6:55	401.3	" Julius	433	f11:06	f10:45
s6:38	s7:14	411.7	" Nenana** (Tanana River)	362	s10:47	s10:28
f6:50	f7:23	415.4	" North Nenana	367	f10:36	f10:10
f6:58	f7:30	420.4	" Berg	368	f10:29	f10:02
f7:15	f7:47	431.6	" Dunbar	368	f10:12	f9:45
f7:28	f7:59	439.5	" Standard	406	f10:00	f9:32
f7:46	f8:16	450.3	" Saulich	465	f9:43	f9:14
f7:56	f8:26	456.2	" Dome	520	f9:33	f9:04
f8:12	f8:41	463.0	" Happy (Gold Dredge)	609	f9:18	f8:48
		467.1	" College (University of Alaska)	436		
s8:30	s8:59	470.3	Ar Fairbanks (Gateway to Arctic) Lv	448	9:00	8:30

REFERENCE NOTES
A.M. time shown in light face type.   s—Station stop   **Telegraph station.
P.M. time shown in **bold face type.**   f—Stops on flag

Construction moved forward, and after the Hurricane Gulch Bridge was finished in August 1921, three of the biggest remaining challenges before finishing the rail line were getting through the Nenana River canyon, building a 900-foot-long bridge over Riley Creek, and building a 701-foot bridge over the Tanana River. The first train from Seward to Nenana ran on February 5, 1922. (Candy Waugaman collection.)

The Alaska Railroad Company installed this welcoming arch in 1926 not far from the McKinley Park Station railroad stop. The arch was situated at the beginning of the park road to welcome visitors. (Candy Waugaman collection.)

From 1922 to 1923, rail passengers could take a ferry across the Tanana River and then get back on the rail line for the rest of the journey to Fairbanks. When work crews finished the bridge over the Tanana River, the rail line was officially complete, and people could ride without stopping to get on a ferry partway through their journey. (Candy Waugaman collection.)

The establishment of a rail line running past Denali provided extra impetus for the creation of the park. Sheldon and other advocates recognized that market hunting would likely increase to feed workers on the rail line as it inched its way past the Alaska Range, and consequently increase the need for a park or a game preserve to protect Dall sheep and other game from possible extinction. (Candy Waugaman collection.)

Charles Sheldon first publicly presented the idea of a game preserve to protect Dall sheep and other wildlife at a meeting of the Boone and Crockett Club in 1909. Once Wickersham became Alaska's nonvoting delegate to Congress—also in 1909—Sheldon found himself with a more powerful political backer. Many Alaskans were actually against the creation of a park because it would limit their mining claims and their ability to hunt in the area. The US government had already made intrusions into their way of life and into Alaskan land—first with passage of the 1908 Alaska Game Law and then with President Taft's withdrawal of oil tracts in 1910. (Candy Waugaman collection.)

Galvanized by Wilson's executive order establishing the new rail line, Sheldon set to work to try to establish the park before rail crews reached the area. On September 21, 1915, he got the Boone and Crockett Club to pass a resolution in support of creating a Mount McKinley National Park. (Candy Waugaman collection.)

In order to get support from more local Alaskans, Wickersham advised Sheldon they would need to propose a park bill that would allow for local mining claims. Sheldon then enlisted the support of Stephen Mather, who was the assistant in charge of national parks to the secretary of the interior, in creating a park to protect the area's game and to preserve the region's beauty for tourists and visitors. (Candy Waugaman collection.)

Sheldon also gained the support of Belmore Browne, who had taken part in three Denali expeditions, and Thomas Riggs, who was the head of the Alaska Engineering Commission and in charge of constructing the railroad to Fairbanks. These three men would confer on the boundaries of the park to propose to Congress. While the park would include mountains in the Alaska Range and the game lands to the north, it would leave out much of the Kantishna Hills even farther north so that local mining claims would not be infringed upon. (Candy Waugaman collection.)

Wickersham submitted a draft of the park bill to the House of Representatives on April 18, 1916. Within the park boundaries, subsistence hunting would be permitted but game hunting, in which the meat is later sold for profit, would be disallowed. President Wilson signed the park bill into law on February 26, 1917. (Candy Waugaman collection.)

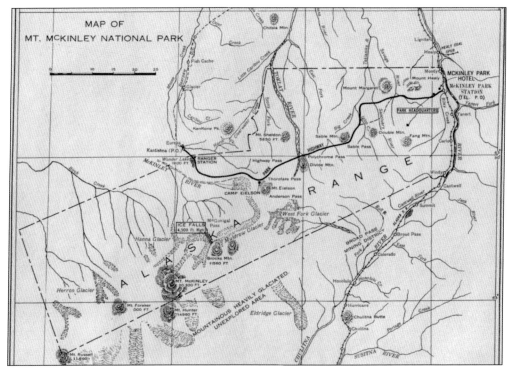

Three different individuals submitted proposal's for the new park's boundaries, including Sheldon, the original proponent of the bill; Thomas Riggs, the head of the Alaska Engineering Commission, which was constructing the Alaska Railroad; and Belmore Browne, who had also had his own plan for promoting a park prior to Sheldon's. Congress ended up going with a version of Riggs's proposal for the park's borders, which omitted parks of Kantishna and thereby left those areas open for mining. (Candy Waugaman collection.)

The new park would encompass nearly 1.6 million acres and protect the many species of mammals and birds that lived in the area from excessive hunting. After the passage of the park bill, the next battle would be to secure funding from the federal government to pay for the park's first rangers. (Candy Waugaman collection.)

At the time the park bill was passed, the railroad was already north of the Matanuska Valley in Alaska and creeping its way toward the outer boundary of the park. The park needed rangers to patrol the area and to make sure game protection was enforced. While the secretary of the interior sent a letter to the secretary of the treasury to ask for $10,000 to fund the new park, the request was temporarily pushed to the side. (Candy Waugaman collection.)

As the railroad made its way north from Seward, it also started to make its way south toward the new park from Fairbanks. By the fall of 1920, the rail line had already reached Healy, just outside of the park boundaries. Sheldon came before Congress on December 16, 1920, to urge the quick appropriation of funding for rangers to patrol the area and prevent the indiscriminate slaughter of wildlife. (Candy Waugaman collection.)

On March 4, 1921, Congress passed the Sundry Civil Bill and appropriated an additional $8,000 for the National Park Service. The next task would be to select the superintendent—and first ranger—to lead and manage Mount McKinley National Park. (Candy Waugaman collection.)

Sheldon favored Harry Karstens as the first superintendent. However, Alaska governor Thomas Riggs wanted W.B. Reaburn, a veteran of the Alaska-Canada Boundary Survey, to fill the post. After considering Karstens, Reaburn, and other candidates, the National Park Service director appointed Karstens as the first superintendent of Mount McKinley National Park. (Candy Waugaman collection.)

The National Park Service director sent Karstens a letter in April 1921 notifying him of his appointment and detailing his duties. His appointment started on July 1, 1921, but he arrived back in Alaska by steamship and started work that June. This image is of a camp during the early days of the park. (Candy Waugaman collection.)

Karstens first established a temporary park headquarters at Nenana. As progress on the Alaska Railroad continued—the bridge over Hurricane Gulch was completed on August 8, and thus a significant obstacle overcome—pressure increased to establish the actual park headquarters. (Candy Waugaman collection.)

The Alaska Engineering Commission selected the site for its rail stop near the park—to be called McKinley Park Station—near Riley Creek in September 1921. Karstens decided on the same

site as the location for the permanent park headquarters and the main entrance to the park for visitors. (Candy Waugaman collection.)

One of the first tasks for Karstens in establishing the fledgling Mount McKinley National Park was the construction of a road, which would allow easy passage for automobiles and access to the park for tourists when they arrived by train at McKinley Park Station. (Candy Waugaman collection.)

As the development of the park moved forward, Karstens began to entertain applications from prospective concessioners who wanted to build a park hotel and run horseback-riding operations. However, these initial proposals came to naught, as some lacked the financial backing to get off the ground and others faltered before they started due to a dearth of tourists actually visiting the park. (Candy Waugaman collection.)

National Park Service director Stephen Mather conferred with Karstens and with the Alaska Road Commission on different proposals for road construction. The first road to be approved would stretch 110 miles from McKinley Park Station to the Kantishna Post Office. The majority of the roadway would be suitable for travel only on horseback or by foot, with 39 miles of the route drivable by automobiles. (Candy Waugaman collection.)

It was not until 1922 that the first tourists began to flow in to the park, and just seven people visited that year. The Alaska Railroad would begin to recruit tourists in earnest in 1924 with Mount McKinley as the main attraction. (Candy Waugaman collection.)

The Alaska Road Commission began to look at building a road to Savage River in 1923. Both National Park Service staff and Alaska Road Commission staff worked on the project. Construction that year cost $4,261. (Candy Waugaman collection.)

On April 9, 1924, Congress passed a bill to fund road construction in national parks for the following three years. The act included $272,200 from National Park Service funds for roads in Mount McKinley National Park. (Candy Waugaman collection.)

Road crews worked through the summer into November 1924. Rather than requesting the road follow the most direct route from McKinley Park Station to Kantishna, federal officials asked the Alaska Road Commission to take a more circuitous path that would allow travelers views of scenic vistas. (Candy Waugaman collection.)

Nearly 90 workers from the Alaska Road Commission helped build the road in 1924. By the end of the season, however, the road only stretched for the first 10 miles and cars were not able to drive on it. Ultimately, it would take until 1938 for the park road to stretch all the way to the Kantishna. (Candy Waugaman collection.)

This image is of Savage Camp in Denali. The availability of cabins at the camp helped to boost tourism in the 1920s. While there were still no official tour operators by the summer of 1922, in 1923 a horse packer named Dan Kennedy—who was also a longtime friend of Karstens—requested the first permit approved by the Department of the Interior. The next major concessioner would be the Mount McKinley Tourist and Transportation Company, which operated from 1925 to 1939. (Candy Waugaman collection.)

The Morino Roadhouse in the park would be attached to the post office. The roadhouse was home to over 20 rooms for travelers, and Maurice Morino, the owner, also served as the local postmaster. In May 1950, someone dropped a lit cigarette on the floor that would ignite a fire and cause the roadhouse to burn down. (Candy Waugaman collection.)

On July 15, 1923, Pres. Warren G. Harding, seen here (second from left) with First Lady Florence Harding, visited Mount McKinley National Park and gave remarks to the press. (Candy Waugaman collection.)

From left to right in this image are First Lady Harding; George Parks, later the governor of Alaska; and Dan Kennedy, one of the first concessioners in the park, during the Hardings' 1923 visit. (Candy Waugaman collection.)

While he was on the Denali trip, President Harding nailed in a golden spike at the Nenana River bridge to symbolize the completion of the Alaska Railroad. The party then continued on to Fairbanks and circled back to Seward. (Candy Waugaman collection.)

While the Alaska Road Commission built the road through the park, the road commission and the National Park Service built a series of simple cabins along the way to house park service rangers. A number of the cabins would also have doghouses and storage caches, such as the one on stilts in this image. (Candy Waugaman collection.)

Savage River Camp and Mt. McKinley - Mt. Kinley Park - Alaska

This photograph is of Savage Camp. It is likely that Alaska Road Commission workers built the first cabins here in 1924 or 1925. The Mount McKinley Tourist and Transportation Company also set up 26 tent houses for visitors. (Candy Waugaman collection.)

Most tourists who visited the camp traveled on horseback. However, miners in the Kantishna area often used dog teams or walked. The first park visitors to enter the park by automobile came in with Karstens behind the wheel in August 1924. (Candy Waugaman collection.)

Karstens bought seven dogs for use by the rangers in February 1922. Later that year, he ordered the first dog kennels built, and from early on in the park's history, rangers employed dog teams to conduct patrols in winter. Pictured above are dog kennels, and seen below is a dog sled garage. (Both, Candy Waugaman collection.)

This photograph shows huskies at Mount McKinley National Park in 1936. Karstens had decided in 1926 to create a new area to house the dogs close to park headquarters and make it easier for tourists to visit the animals. (Candy Waugaman collection.)

Dan T. Kennedy standing by Location Monument Mt. Hayes Landing Field

Dan Kennedy, shown here at Mount Hayes Landing Field, received a permit to be the park's first concessioner in the summer of 1923. He had previously operated a successful freighting company for miners on the Richardson Trail. (Candy Waugaman collection.)

Dan T. Kennedy scouting for Aeroplane Landing Fields East and West Forks Dry Delta vicinity of Mt. Hayes in July 1930

This photograph shows Dan Kennedy scouting for landing fields near Mount Hayes in 1930. After selling his own freight business, he would do contract hauling for the Alaska Engineering Commission. One reason Kennedy pursued the park concession is that there was decreasing demand for independent freighters because of the railroad. (Candy Waugaman collection.)

Under the terms of the permit described in the letter here from Kennedy to Karstens, Kennedy had permission to establish three camps in the park. He was also required to supply 30 horses for tourist operations. (Candy Waugaman collection.)

Nenana, Alaska.
Jan. 4,1925.

Mr. Harry P. Karstens,
Supt. Mt. McKinley National Park,
McKinley Park, Alaska.

Sir:-

I hereby request permission to operate pack trains through the Mt. McKinley National Park, for the accomodation of tourists, transportation of supplies and equipment etc.

I agree to maintain thirty head of stock with complete rigging and equipment which will enable me to care for tourist parties in reasonable numbers, and will furnish additional stock to take care of any increase in the trade.

I will also furnish competent guides and packers with each outfit, and will endeavor to co-operate with the Park Service in every way possible for the betterment of the accommodations at all times.

If no plans for the hotel or road house accomodations of the travellers has been made I will furnish necessary camp equipment and cooks until such provision is made.

If the above plans are satisfactory I request that the privilege be granted for a minimum time of ten years.

Very respectfully yours,
Dan T. Kennedy

The above permit approved by me.
Henry P. Karstens
Supt

Karstens, whose camp is featured in this image, immediately started to butt heads with Kennedy, who supplied 15 horses instead of the 30 he agreed to and frequently used shabby, secondhand equipment. (Candy Waugaman collection.)

This photograph is of Karstens's camp at Riley Creek. Kennedy also did not finish work on Savage Camp in time for a visit by a Congressional delegation on July 7, 1923, which forced Karstens to hold the ceremony at McKinley Park Station instead of at the camp. (Candy Waugaman collection.)

Memoranda of instances covering alleged inefficiency
of Supt. Karstens of Mt. McKinley National Park, and also the
lack of support and co-operation given by him to Dan T. Kennedy,
Manager, The Mt. McKinley Tourist and Transportation Co.

1. A telegram from the National Park Service at
Washington, dated December 11, 1922 to Supt. Karstens, instruct-
ing him to investigate and get formal written application for a
transportation concession in the Park was not communicated to
Kennedy until January 3, 1923. Karstens knew Kennedy was at
Nenana and could have been readily reached by telephone.
(Exhibit #1)

Later Karstens wired Kennedy - 170 words, collect
$8.77, an unnecessarily expensive telegram - after Kennedy had
gone to the States. Trouble was experienced in getting into
communication with Karstens and there was delay in forwarding
necessary papers. Karstens' dilatory methods and his lack of
ordinary business enterprise made the extra trip back to Alaska
necessary, at heavy expense of time and money.
(Exhibit #2)

2.
Karstens' letter of July 12, 1923, stating that Kennedy has but one large tent installed at Savage River Camp, was
not true. This letter also gives further evidence of Karstens'
tendency to handicap and harass Kennedy in his operations.
(Exhibit #3)

A reply to this letter, by Kennedy, accompanied by
photographs, shows that there was much other tentage in service
at Savage River camp besides the one referred to in Karstens'
letter. Kennedy's reply to Karstens' letter answers other
charges made.
(Exhibit #4)

3. A schedule of rates approved by the National Park
Service at Washington appears to have been received by Karstens
on June 2, 1923, but was not communicated to Kennedy until June
29th. At this season it was very important that such information
be made known at once.

4. Although there was an entire absence of roads into
the Park in June 1923, Karstens prevailed upon Kennedy to go to
the expense of shipping three stages from Fairbanks to McKinley
Park at a cost of about $150.00 for freight, loading and unload-
ing. After their impracticability had been demonstrated, Karstens shipped the stages back to Fairbanks on Government bill-of-
lading.

Only 34 tourists came to visit Kennedy's camp in 1923. Karstens accused Kennedy of failing to do what he agreed to in the permit, and Kennedy said that Karstens did not give him enough support for tourism operations. This "memorandum of inefficiency" details Kennedy's accusations against Karstens. (Candy Waugaman collection.)

Construction of the Wonder Lake Ranger Station, located at the end of the road, started in 1939. Supt. Frank Been directed the project and employed Civilian Conservation Corps workers to begin construction in June. (Library of Congress.)

By September 1939, the five-room ranger station was complete and ready for year-round occupancy, with electricity and running water. District Ranger John Rumohr and Ranger Raymond McIntyre occupied the station and conducted winter patrols for its inaugural winter of 1939–1940. This image is of the living room and dining room at the station. (Library of Congress.)

After the winter of 1939–1940, the Wonder Lake Ranger Station would be used only for summer housing. The front room (pictured) was where visitors could enter and consult with the rangers. This was the main station for rangers to oversee the western side of the park. (Library of Congress.)

In the winter of 1947–1948, a grizzly bear broke in to the station. The bear ate through the food supplies stored in the basement, spilled a bucket of paint, and tore the doors off of cupboards. The next season, National Park Service staff did not store food at the station in order to prevent such mishaps. (Library of Congress.)

In 1964 and in 1967, the National Park Service added new cabins outside the Wonder Lake Ranger Station for lodging. In 1998, park staff discovered that the main building was resting on top of an ice lens that shifted seasonally and caused problems with the station's structural stability. In order to ameliorate the problem, the upper building was moved so that the basement could be filled in, and then the building was placed back in the original location. (Library of Congress.)

Flight seeing was one activity available to tourists early on in the park's history. In the summer of 1930, Mount McKinley Tourism and Transportation Company got a permit from the National Park Service to operate planes from Savage Camp to fly tourists for views of the mountain and to different points of interest throughout the park. (Candy Waugaman collection.)

Following Dan Kennedy's tenure, the park hired Mount McKinley Tourist and Transportation Company to serve as park concessioner. The company would run tourism operations from June 17, 1925, until June 1, 1939. (Candy Waugaman collection.)

The Mount McKinley Tourist and Transportation Company was the first concessioner to operate buses to transport tourists into the park. This c. 1939 image features Robert "Bobby" Sheldon, the general manager for the Richardson Highway Transportation Company, who oversaw tourism operations at Savage Camp. (DENA 22125.)

Pictured, from left to right, are Harry Liek, Grant Pearson, Erling Strom, and Al Lindley in front of McKinley Park Station in 1932. The group had just made the second ascent of Denali's south peak and also climbed the north peak in the same trip. Liek served as park superintendent from November 1928 to May 1939, when Frank Been succeeded him. (DENA 3966.)

Grant Pearson was hired as a temporary park ranger in the winter of 1926. Pearson was originally from Michigan and had worked for the Alaska Road Commission. When he heard about an opening for a temporary ranger in a letter from McKinley ranger Albert Winn, Pearson applied for and received the job, and then moved up through the ranks. (Candy Waugaman collection.)

Winn then trained Grant Pearson, pictured here at Toklat in 1954, on how to mush dogs and how to stop poachers while on patrol. When Winn resigned, Pearson was able to leave his position as temporary ranger to take Winn's slot as a permanent ranger. (DENA 2355.)

This is the interior of the Pearson Cabin, also known as the Toklat Patrol Cabin, which Pearson and Lee Swisher built in 1927. Grant Pearson would become acting park superintendent in February 1943, and was elected to be a member of the new state legislature during Alaska's last days as a US territory in 1958. (Library of Congress.)

This image of Grant Pearson (left) and Harold Booth was made when Pearson was superintendent and Booth was a park ranger. Apart from helping to build cabins, Pearson also helped with the construction of park headquarters before becoming superintendent. (DENA 4844.)

Grant Pearson was nearly killed in a blizzard while on patrol in 1927. Superintendent Karstens then ordered an extensive series of cabins, similar to the Pearson Cabin pictured here, to be constructed so that rangers would have access to shelter while on patrol. Pearson helped gather the lumber for the cabins. (Library of Congress.)

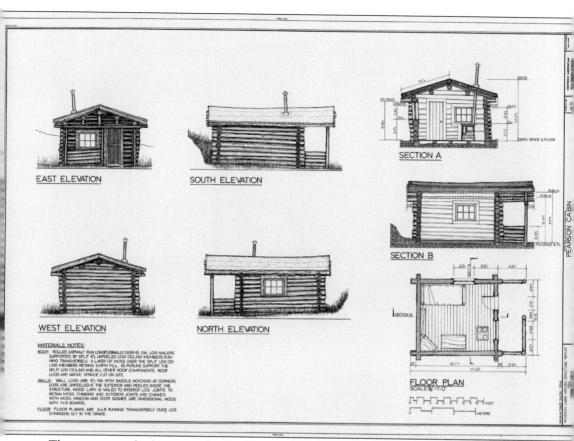

The ranger-patrol cabins were simple affairs—often just a single room with an entryway. Building a cabin could take weeks because rangers not only had to cut the lumber themselves but also had to haul it to the construction site using dog teams. (Library of Congress.)

Sometimes, rangers would make improvements to patrol cabins by building storage caches, such as the one in this image, or by adding outhouses or dog shelters. The resulting cabins were significantly more hospitable than the tents rangers had previously relied on during frigid Alaskan winters. (Library of Congress.)

Adolph Murie, pictured here in 1965 at the East Fork Cabin with his wife, Louise Murie, held a master's of science and a doctorate in natural science from the University of Michigan. He first came to the park in 1922 when he was an undergraduate student to assist his brother Olaus Murie, a biologist, with collecting specimens of caribou for the US Biological Survey. (DENA 22850.)

To collect the caribou specimens alive, Olaus and Adolph Murie would drive them into a corral, where they would lasso and hog-tie the animals to keep them separated. Adolph is pictured here at Igloo Canyon. (DENA 22782.)

This photograph of Adolph Murie's living quarters dates from March 1950. Murie would work for the National Park Service for nearly 32 years and become a renowned researcher of wolves and Dall sheep. (DENA 21428.)

This is an image of Adolph Murie's daughter, Gail, in an East Fork wolf den. Murie's research on mammals in Denali would cause controversy because, contrary to the trend at the time to study each species individually, he focused on the ecosystem as a whole and treated each individual species as just one piece of the puzzle. (DENA 22307.)

Mrs. D.R. Murdock, the daughter of Charles Sheldon, is seen here talking with Adolph Murie near the Sanctuary River Cabin during her first visit to the park in August 1966. Murie earned the Distinguished Service Award from the National Park Service, and the National Park Service dedicated the Murie Science and Learning Center to him in 2004. (DENA 22855.)

Louise Murie, Adolph Murie's wife, stands in this image with a wolf in Denali. Adolph authored a book called *The Wolves of Mount McKinley* in 1944. He also authored four other books—*Mammals of Denali, The Ecology of the Coyote in Yellowstone, A Naturalist in Alaska,* and *The Grizzlies of Mount McKinley.* (DENA 22779.)

Adolph Murie is third from left in the back row in this photograph of park staff. Murie and his family moved to Jackson Hole, Wyoming, in 1945. He died on August 16, 1974, in Moose, Wyoming. (DENA 22724.)

This tourist brochure created by the Department of the Interior, which managed the National Park Service, dates from 1940. The Alaska Railroad, which managed the park hotel, was the main tourism concessioner at this time. (Candy Waugaman collection.)

RULES AND REGULATIONS
[Briefed]

The Park Regulations are designed for the protection of the natural beauties and scenery as well as for the comfort and convenience of visitors. Complete regulations may be examined at the office of the superintendent of the park. The following synopsis is for the general guidance of visitors, who are requested to assist in the administration of the park by observing the rules.

The destruction, defacement, or disturbance of buildings, signs, equipment, or other property, or of trees, flowers, vegetation, or other natural conditions and curiosities is prohibited.

Camping with tents is permitted. When in the vicinity of designated camp sites these sites must be used. Only dead and down timber should be used for fuel. All refuse should be burned or buried.

Fires shall be lighted only when necessary, and when no longer needed shall be completely extinguished. They shall not be built in duff or a location where a conflagration may result. No lighted cigar, cigarette, or other burning material shall be dropped in any grass, twigs, leaves, or tree mold.

All hunting, killing, wounding, frightening, capturing, or attempting to capture any wild bird or animal is prohibited. Firearms are prohibited in the park except with the permission of the superintendent.

Fishing in any manner other than with hook and line is prohibited. Fishing in particular waters may be suspended by the superintendent.

Cameras may be freely used in the park for general scenic picture purposes.

Gambling in any form or the operation of gambling devices, whether for merchandise or otherwise, is prohibited.

Private notices or advertisements shall not be posted or displayed in the park, excepting such as the superintendent deems necessary for the convenience and guidance of the public.

Dogs are not permitted in the park, except by special permission of the superintendent.

Mountain climbing shall be undertaken only with permission of the superintendent.

The penalty for violation of the rules and regulations is a fine of not more than $500, or imprisonment not exceeding 6 months, or both, together with all costs of the proceedings.

W. H. Kistler Stationery Co., Denver, Colorado. 2-20-40—22M.

These are the park regulations in the brochure provided to tourists entering the park. True to the goals of Sheldon and other early park advocates, the rules prohibit any kind of hunting or trapping of wildlife. (Candy Waugaman collection.)

This photograph is of members of the Harvard Mountaineering Club in August 1952. The club started in 1924 and focused on mountains far from Cambridge, Massachusetts—such as those in the Canadian Rockies, the European Alps, and the Himalayas. Bradford Washburn was one well-known climber to come up through the ranks of this club. (DENA 22235.)

Four

MILITARY INFLUENCE AND THE TOURISM BOOM

Once the United States joined the fight in World War II, the US military had an increasing interest in Alaska as a strategic location. In 1942, members of both the American and Canadian militaries took part in the US Army Alaska Testing Expedition to test out cold-weather gear and practice survival skills. Several members of the expedition are featured here traveling across a glacier. (DENA 22271.)

Members of the US Army Alaska Testing Expedition are shown here amidst a glacial moraine, which is rock and debris picked up by the glacier and deposited at its edge. Seventeen people participated in the testing expedition, which lasted six weeks. (DENA 22272.)

Pictured are, from left to right, Col. Frank Marchman, Supt. Frank Been, Terris Moore, Grant Pearson, and Bradford Washburn. Originally from Boston, Washburn began exploring and climbing mountains in Alaska by the 1930s and achieved a number of notable first ascents, including the first climb of the West Buttress route on Denali, the route the majority of climbers attempt today. He would also create an authoritative map of Denali that climbers use to this day. Washburn assisted with the expedition because of his intimate knowledge of the Alaska Range after doing aerial reconnaissance. (DENA 22287.)

The group traveled across the Muldrow Glacier and made its camp close to McGonagall Pass. National Park Service rangers would make trips up to the camp to resupply the soldiers during their stay. (DENA 22273.)

This image is of the soldiers' campsite at McGonagall Pass during the 1942 testing expedition. During the trip, they tested skis, food, tents, parachutes, and other gear. Apart from testing cold-weather gear, seven men in the group—including Bradford Washburn—completed a Denali summit climb on July 23 and 24. (DENA 22281.)

For the summit climb, the group approached the mountain by the Muldrow Glacier and the Harper Glacier—the same route as the Sourdough Expedition. Its climb marked the third ascent of Denali's south peak. (DENA 22286.)

Three big developments came out of the 1942 test expedition: the park service received a major equipment donation, the military made decisions on what gear was and was not appropriate for soldiers potentially facing cold environments, and the military began to examine the idea of using the park as a recreation site for off-duty soldiers. (DENA 22280.)

During the expedition, army mountaineers would strap crampons like these to the bottoms of their boots for traction on hard-packed ice and snow. In the early 1900s, climbers referred to crampons as "ice-creepers"; today, *crampons* is the accepted term used. (DENA 22286.)

Apart from the 1942 test expedition, military personnel also used mountaineering skills to participate in rescue missions. In September 1944, a plane with 19 people on board—including the son of a congressman—crashed in the park, and Army officials immediately began to look at mounting a rescue at the crash site. (Candy Waugaman collection.)

Even though aerial reconnaissance suggested there were no survivors of the crash, the military asked Pearson to organize a rescue mission. When he declined, officials threatened to draft him, so he then organized a 44-person rescue party. (Candy Waugaman collection.)

Pearson took his massive team to Wonder Lake to get on the Muldrow Glacier and start the rescue mission. He whittled the team he would take to the crash site down to just 12 men and got Bradford Washburn to help lead the group. While the party was not able to find the bodies of the passengers beneath the deep snowdrifts, all clues at the crash site suggested there were no survivors. (Candy Waugaman collection.)

Shortly after the rescue mission, Washburn returned to lead military personnel on another cold-weather testing expedition. This image is from one of the cold-weather trips the military mounted. After two months of testing gear on the Muldrow Glacier and the West Fork Glacier, Washburn and his men concluded their trip on December 6, 1944. (DENA 22276.)

CROSSING THE ALASKA RANGE
—ALASKA—

In the 1950s, tourism providers began to look at increasing air service to the park. Mount McKinley Tourist and Transportation Company built a landing strip at Savage Camp in 1930, but there had been little development of air travel for tourism since that time. (Candy Waugaman collection.)

Airstrips were built outside, but with easy access to, the park in Cantwell, Crooked Creek, and Glen Creek in the 1950s and 1960s. Some of these sites were used for mining rather than tourism. (DENA 22285.)

In 1934, the Department of the Interior began to give a serious look at building at least one hotel in the park. The government considered sites near McKinley Park Station and at Mile 66 along the park road, and the idea of a hotel near the station naturally received huge support from the Alaska Railroad. (Candy Waugaman collection.)

Secretary of the Interior Harold Ickes initially approved $350,000 from Works Progress Administration funds to go toward construction of the McKinley Park Hotel. The building site, approximately 300 yards from McKinley Park Station, was surveyed in May 1937. (Candy Waugaman collection.)

The Department of the Interior announced construction on June 20, 1937, and by August, 78 people were working on the project. Construction ended in late November and began again the next April. (Candy Waugaman collection.)

The hotel ultimately faced a turbulent road toward completion. Ickes came to inspect the project and found it not to his satisfaction—the rooms were too uncomfortable and received little light. He ordered the construction of a new 46-room wing and a larger dining hall. Construction continued through the winter until the summer of 1939. (Candy Waugaman collection.)

The McKinley Park Hotel opened for business on June 1, 1939, and was part of a larger plan to encourage tourism and economic development in the area. It had the capacity to house 200 guests and cost between $300,000 and $450,000 all told. (Candy Waugaman collection.)

The summer the hotel opened saw tourism increase by more than 50 percent, up from 1,487 visitors to 2,262. During World War II, the majority of visitors would be US military personnel; in December 1941, the US Department of War banned civilian travel to Alaska for tourism because of the state's proximity to Asia. (Candy Waugaman collection.)

The park was an official US Army "recreation camp" from April 1943 to March 1945 and primarily served military personnel stationed in Alaska. The military would use the park again as a "recreational rest camp" for the winter seasons during the Korean War. (Candy Waugaman collection.)

513 Horseshoe Lake – McKinley Park

Two tourists stand here in front of Horseshoe Lake. Among the first trails in the park, the path to here is a 1.5-mile trek from the park hotel. In the mid-1940s, military personnel could go to

the lake for ice-skating and were also able to go dog mushing, try archery, and even ski using a ski tow set up at Mile 6 of the road. (Candy Waugaman collection.)

MOUNT McKINLEY LODGE
McKinley National Park

The park began its transition from military to civilian tourism just two months after the armistice with Japan. In 1945, tourists could get to Alaska by steamship or by commercial air, and by 1948 travelers could get there using the new Alaska-Canada Highway, known as the Alcan. However, steamship remained the primary mode of travel to Alaska and maritime labor strikes, plus the fact that many ships had been requisitioned by the government during World War II, stymied efforts to increase tourism immediately following the war. (Candy Waugaman collection.)

This photograph of Joe Hankins was taken in 1971. Hankins served as host of Igloo Campground. As an amateur naturalist, he would give talks to tourists from the 1950s through the 1970s. (DENA 23122.)

This image is of a Tundra Wildlife Tour Bus at Stony Overlook (Mile 61.4 on the park road). Park concessioners offered tourism-oriented wildlife bus tours starting in the 1940s and also operated a separate shuttle bus system for the National Park Service. (Candy Waugaman collection.)

There was a sharp uptick in backpacking and hiking in the park in early 1970s. Starting in 1971, backpackers were allowed to use buses to get to different points along the park road, and the number of backcountry visitors nearly doubled, from 5,419 in 1971 to 10,437 to 1973. (Candy Waugaman collection.)

Park visitation as a whole rose sharply in the 1970s. Some 160,600 people came to the park in 1975, compared to 21,406 visitors in 1965. The number of park visitors would continue to rise in the coming decade. (Candy Waugaman collection.)

Five

MODERN CLIMBING

Denali is just one of hundreds of mountains in the Alaska Range to offer challenges to climbers. The first ascent of Mount Foraker, which stands at 17,400 feet tall, took place in 1934 and is described by Charles Houston, the team's leader, in the *American Alpine Journal* in 1935. Apart from the more moderate Sultana Ridge route, Mount Foraker also features a climb called the Infinite Spur. (Candy Waugaman collection.)

The Infinite Spur consists of 9,000 feet of rock, snow, and ice climbing. Alex Bertulis and a partner made the first attempt by this route in 1968, and George Lowe and Michael Kennedy made the first successful ascent in 1977. Their climb took over seven days, and they gave it its name for the way it seemed to continue on forever. ("Carol M. Highsmith's America," Library of Congress, Prints & Photographs Division.)

The Sultana Ridge on Mount Foraker offers a far more moderate route up the mountain than the Infinite Spur. Nevertheless, any Mount Foraker climb is a remote experience without the support of National Park Service rangers. (Author's collection.)

One popular climbing area in the Alaska Range is the Ruth Gorge, with its towering alpine spires carved out by the Ruth Glacier. Among other routes, there are climbs on a series of spires called the Bear Tooth, the Moose's Tooth, the Eye Tooth, the Broken Tooth, and the Sugar Tooth. ("Carol M. Highsmith's America," Library of Congress, Prints & Photographs Division.)

The Ruth Gorge fills the lower part of the frame with Denali in the background. A number of alpine test pieces are scattered throughout the Ruth Gorge, including Ham and Eggs and Shaken, Not Stirred on the Moose's Tooth. (Candy Waugaman collection.)

American Sue Nott and Karen McNeill, a Canadian, accomplished the first female ascent of the Cassin Ridge, one of the most challenging routes on Denali, in 2004. They carried enough

food for four days but ended up spending eight on the route after a one-day approach. ("Carol M. Highsmith's America," Library of Congress, Prints & Photographs Division.)

In May 2006, McNeill and Nott returned to Alaska to attempt the Infinite Spur on Mount Foraker. They carried enough food for two weeks but did not return on schedule. After three weeks, the National Park Service launched a search but failed to find the missing climbers. While some of their gear was discovered, what happened to the two women remains a mystery. ("Carol M. Highsmith's America," Library of Congress, Prints & Photographs Division.)

Mount Hunter stands at 14,573 feet and is home to challenging routes, such as the Moonflower, and to more moderate climbs. The Moonflower consists of 6,100 feet of rock and ice climbing. Pat Klewin, Doug Klewin, and Todd Bibler made the first attempt on this route in 1979. ("Carol M. Highsmith's America," Library of Congress, Prints & Photographs Division.)

After the Klewin and Bibler attempt, Mugs Stump and Paul Aubrey were the first to successfully climb the route in 1980 but did not continue on to Mount Hunter's summit. In 1984, Rob Newsome and Pat McNerthney were the first to climb the Moonflower and then reach the summit. ("Carol M. Highsmith's America," Library of Congress, Prints & Photographs Division.)

This mountain on the Pika Glacier is called The Throne. This peak stands at 7,390 feet and features a multitude of rock routes; climbers started putting routes up in the 1970s. A popular rock route called The Lost Marsupial follows the west rock rib up to the summit, and its first known ascent was in 1996. (Author's collection.)

One hazard climbers occasionally encounter during glacier travel is this feature called a moulin. These pools of water lead deep down into the glacier and are incredibly dangerous because if someone falls in, he or she can be sucked down. ("Carol M. Highsmith's America," Library of Congress, Prints & Photographs Division.)

Here, a team moves on skis across the Pika Glacier in the Alaska Range. Climbers must travel roped together on a glacier in order to be able to rescue one another if someone falls in a crevasse. Traveling roped up can also provide extra protection from a fall on steep snow slopes. (Author's collection.)

In order to travel safely on a glaciated mountain like Denali, climbers must possess strong crevasse rescue skills. Here, Hana Beaman practices pulling Robert Foreman out of a crevasse during a simulated crevasse rescue scenario on Mount Baker, in Washington State. Many climbers hone their skills on peaks like Mounts Baker or Rainier in the Cascades before coming to the Alaska Range. (Author's collection.)

There are multiple systems for pulling a fallen climber out of a crevasse. Here, Hana Beaman practices what is known as a Z-pulley system. She buries long metal stakes, called pickets, in the snow for an anchor and uses the rope to rig a haul system to pull her partner out. (Author's collection.)

Robert Foreman takes a rest during crevasse rescue practice. Climbers not only need to be able to rescue their partners, but they must also have self-rescue skills. If a climber falls in, he or she should be able to ascend the rope and escape the crevasse using a friction hitch system. (Author's collection.)

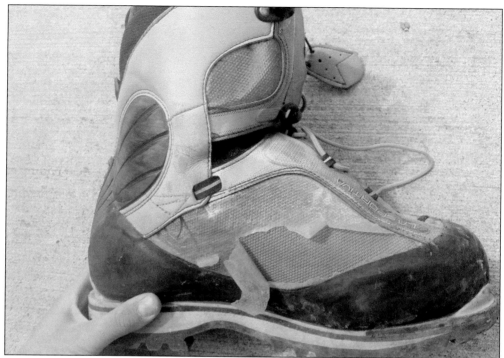

Denali climbers wear double-plastic boots, like these La Sportiva Spantiks, which include an inner boot of foam that insulates and an outer boot of hard plastic that blocks out any moisture. Once they reach 17,200 feet, climbers must also put on an overboot of neoprene for extra insulation. (Author's collection.)

Depending on the area where they are going, climbers have the option either to climb on their own or to hire a guide to lead them. Guide Winslow Passey prepares to fly in to the Alaska Range to instruct climbers on a 12-day mountaineering course. (Author's collection.)

Mountain guide Hugh Gaasch (left) and mountaineering student Steve Roylance wait for a ski-equipped plane to pick them up on the Pika Glacier. Climbers fly in and out of the Alaska Range on small single-engine fixed-wing planes, like the Cessna 185, the de Havilland Beaver, or the de Havilland Otter. (Author's collection.)

West Buttress climbers fly in to a central base camp on the Kahiltna Glacier. When climbers return after their ascent to fly out, they coordinate with the base camp manager who connects them with an outgoing flight. Here, climber Rob Litsenberger (right) has just landed at base camp for the first time and chats with the manager (left). The man in the center is unidentified. (Author's collection.)

Here, Rob Litsenberger enjoys a break Denali's lower Kahiltna Glacier. For a standard three-week West Buttress trip, climbers must haul over 100 pounds of gear divided between a backpack and sleds they rig up and drag behind. (Author's collection.)

Climbers follow an established route all the way from the base camp to the summit of Denali. Because over 1,000 climbers attempt the route each year, there is usually an established trail of boot prints in the snow. The route is also often marked with bamboo wands. (Author's collection.)

West Buttress climber Ryan Jones takes a break in his cook tent. While traveling on a glacier, climbers do not have access to running water and must use stoves to melt snow. On the West Buttress, many teams dig kitchens in the snow and set up pyramid-style cook tents overhead in order to cook out of the elements. (Author's collection.)

During a multi-week expedition like the West Buttress, climbers typically use white gas stoves for cooking. It is sometimes difficult to eat higher on the mountain, as nausea is a common symptom of mild altitude illness. Here, David Lynch serves himself food in his cook tent during a West Buttress trip. (Author's collection.)

The 11,000-foot camp on Denali is in a basin below a steep slope called Motorcycle Hill. After ascending Motorcycle Hill and another steep slope called Squirrel Hill, climbers must navigate past Windy Corner, where they pass between a precipitous drop on their right and towering rock face on their left. (Author's collection.)

Climbers Rob Litsenberger (left) and Ryan Jones dig their tents out of the snow on the West Buttress. When climbers get hammered with snow and hard weather, they must shovel out their tents to avoid getting buried and asphyxiated. (Author's collection.)

In order to move their hundreds of pounds of gear up the mountain, climbers will often ferry loads between camps using what is known as a double-carry system. A team will move half of its gear up to the next camp, return to the earlier camp to sleep, and then carry the rest of its gear up the following day. To leave gear at each of the camps, climbers must dig into the snow, bury it, and mark it with wands. (Author's collection.)

Denali's 14,000-foot camp rests in a dramatic basin that ends in a steep drop-off. Here, climbers get spectacular views of Mounts Foraker and Hunter before they climb up fixed lines to move to the next camp at 17,200 feet. (Author's collection.)

This is one of the many cook tents at 14,000 feet on Denali in June 2012. There are often 100 climbers or more at the 14,000-foot camp, given its safe location and the fact that it is a good spot to stop and acclimatize before moving up for a summit attempt. (Author's collection.)

Climbers can get weathered in at camps along the West Buttress route for days—or even for a week or longer—and must come up with creative ways to pass the time. In the summer of 2012, this group of climbers built a clock tower out of snow and established a town square at the 14,000-foot camp. (Author's collection.)

While climbers typically fly in or fly out of the West Buttress on fixed-wing ski-equipped planes, helicopters sometimes come into play in emergencies. Certain helicopters can fly as high as the 14,000-foot and 17,200-foot camps to assist in rescues and pull injured climbers off the mountain. (Author's collection.)

At Denali's 14,000-foot camp, climbers can make a short walk to a rock outcropping called "The Edge of the World," where climber Ryan Jones stands in this image, to get a clear view across the Alaska Range and stand over a drop-off of thousands of feet down onto the Kahiltna Glacier. (Author's collection.)

Above the 14,000-foot camp on Denali are approximately 1,000 feet of rope fixed to the mountain with pickets. Most climbers move up these lines by clipping in to the rope with mechanical ascenders. Here, Spanish climber Iker Bueno speeds past the fixed lines by climbing without clipping in. (Author's collection.)

A rope team is seen in the distance on the Kahiltna Glacier. After summiting, climbers return down the West Buttress, travel across the lower Kahiltna (with stunning views of Mount Foraker along the way), and return to base camp for their flights out. The very last challenge is a 500-foot slope called Heartbreak Hill, which climbers must ascend to reach base camp and conclude their journeys. (Author's collection.)

BIBLIOGRAPHY

Beckey, Fred. *Mount McKinley: Icy Crown of North America.* Seattle: The Mountaineers, 1993.

Berton, Pierre. *Klondike Fever: The Life and Death of the Last Great Gold Rush.* New York: Carroll & Graf Publishers, 2004.

Bryant, Jane. *Snapshots from the Past: A Roadside History of Denali National Park and Preserve.* Denali National Park: Center for Resources, Science & Learning, 2011.

Haigh, Jane G. *Searching for Fannie Quigley: A Wilderness Life in the Shadow of Mount McKinley.* Athens, OH: Swallow Press, 2007.

Martel, Lynn. *Expedition to the Edge: Stories of Worldwide Adventure.* Custer, WA: Rocky Mountain Books, 2008.

Moore, Terris. *Mt. McKinley: The Pioneer Climbs.* Seattle: Mountaineers, 2000.

Norris, Frank. *Crown Jewel of the North: An Administrative History of Denali National Park and Preserve, Volume 1.* Anchorage: Alaska Regional Office, National Park Service, 2006.

Walker, Tom. *Kantishna: Mushers, Miners, Mountaineers—The Pioneer Story Behind Mount McKinley National Park.* Missoula, MT: Pictorial Histories Publishing Co., 2005.

———. *McKinley Station: The People of the Pioneer Park that Became Denali.* Missoula, MT: Pictorial Histories Publishing Co., 2009.

———. *The Seventymile Kid: The Lost Legacy of Harry Karstens and the First Ascent of Mount McKinley.* Seattle: Mountaineers Books, 2013.

Waterman, Laura and Guy Waterman. *Yankee Rock & Ice: A History of Climbing in the Northeastern United States.* Mechanicsburg, PA: Stackpole Books, 1993.

Wood, Michael and Colby Coombs. *Alaska: A Climbing Guide.* Seattle: Mountaineers Books, 2001.

Discover Thousands of Local History Books Featuring Millions of Vintage Images

Arcadia Publishing, the leading local history publisher in the United States, is committed to making history accessible and meaningful through publishing books that celebrate and preserve the heritage of America's people and places.

Find more books like this at
www.arcadiapublishing.com

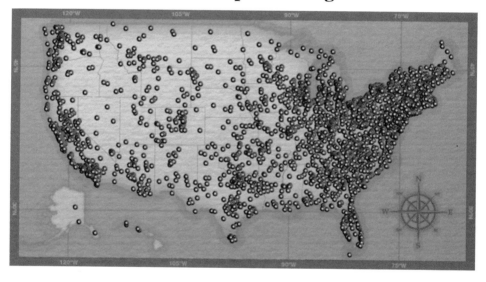

Search for your hometown history, your old stomping grounds, and even your favorite sports team.

Consistent with our mission to preserve history on a local level, this book was printed in South Carolina on American-made paper and manufactured entirely in the United States. Products carrying the accredited Forest Stewardship Council (FSC) label are printed on 100 percent FSC-certified paper.

MADE IN THE USA